Caring for Your
Salamander

Tatiana Tomljanovic

Weigl Publishers Inc.

Project Coordinator
Heather C. Hudak

Design
Warren Clark

Published by Weigl Publishers Inc.
350 5th Avenue, Suite 3304, PMB 6G
New York, NY 10118-0069
Web site: www.weigl.com

Library of Congress Cataloging-in-Publication Data

Tomljanovic, Tatiana.
 Caring for your salamander / by Tatiana Tomljanovic.
    p. cm. -- (Caring for your pet)
 Includes index.
 ISBN 1-59036-476-7 (lib. bdg. : alk. paper) -- ISBN 1-59036-477-5 (soft cover : alk. paper)
 1. Salamanders as pets--Juvenile literature. I. Title. II. Series: Caring for your pet (Mankato, Minn.)
 SF459.S32T66 2006
 639.3'785--dc22

                                2006016105

               Printed in the United States of America
               1 2 3 4 5 6 7 8 9 0   10 09 08 07 06

Locate the salamander footprints throughout the book to find useful tips on caring for your pet.

Photograph and Text Credits
Every reasonable effort has been made to trace ownership and to obtain permission to reprint copyright material. The publishers would be pleased to have any errors or omissions brought to their attention so that they may be corrected in subsequent printings.

Cover: The red-spotted newt is the strongest newt found in North America.

All of the Internet URLs given in the book were valid at the time of publication. However, due to the dynamic nature of the Internet, some addresses may have changed, or sites may have ceased to exist since publication. While the author and publisher regret any inconvenience this may cause readers, no responsibility for any such changes can be accepted by either the author or the publisher.

Contents

Slick Salamanders

Salamanders are a type of amphibian. They are related to frogs and toads. Amphibians live in water and on land. They are **cold-blooded** animals that have a backbone. They do not have hair, feathers, or scales.

It is rare to see salamanders in nature because they are shy and like to hide. Keeping a salamander as a pet allows you to watch him every day. Owners must be patient because even pet salamanders enjoy hiding. Do not startle a salamander with loud noises or quick movements. Be quiet and still, and you can glimpse the life of this unique creature.

Salamanders are expert escape artists. Most can fit through a hole 0.25 inch (0.5 centimeter) wide.

■ For many people, salamanders make interesting pets.

Pet salamanders are easy to care for. They do not need to be brushed, bathed, or walked. They also do not need to be fed every day. Although salamanders are easier to care for than some pets, they are still a big responsibility. Owners must make sure salamanders are healthy and happy by giving them a cool, wet place to live. With proper care, a pet salamander can live a long time.

■ The California newt lives in the coastal mountain ranges between San Diego and Mendocino County, California.

Fascinating Facts

- In nature, salamanders often live in places where the ground is wet and shady. They may hide under logs or rocks near streams.
- Most salamanders feel moist or slimy.
- The largest salamander is the Japanese giant salamander. It grows to about 5 feet (1.5 meters) long.

Pet Profiles

Many factors will affect the type of salamander you choose as a pet. Some salamanders are aquatic. They live in the water. Other salamanders are terrestrial. They live on land. There are also salamanders that spend time both in the water and on land.

TIGER SALAMANDER	FIRE SALAMANDER	CALIFORNIA NEWT

TIGER SALAMANDER
- Terrestrial
- Grows to about 12 inches (30 cm) long
- Thick-bodied
- Color is black with yellow stripes or splotches
- Can live as long as 25 years
- Less shy than other salamanders; will eat from a person's hand

FIRE SALAMANDER
- Terrestrial
- Grows to about 5 to 12 inches (12 to 30 cm) long
- Color is black with bright yellow or orange spots
- Can live as long as 50 years
- Less shy than other salamanders; may follow their owner

CALIFORNIA NEWT
- Aquatic and terrestrial
- Grows to about 7 inches (18 cm) long
- Long, skinny body
- Color is black to reddish brown
- Lives the first part of its life in water, the second part on land, and the final part in the water

Aquatic salamanders need to be kept in a tank with water. This is called an aquarium. Terrestrial salamanders must be kept in a tank without water, called a terrarium.

Salamanders come in many colors, shapes, and sizes. It is important to know how big your salamander could grow. The aquarium or terrarium must be large enough to house the type of salamander you buy.

CAVE SALAMANDER

- Terrestrial
- Grows to 4 to 6 inches (10 to 15 cm)
- Large, thin body
- Eye color is bronze
- Colors range from yellow to bright red with dark spots all over its body
- Lives in or near caves that have water

MEXICAN AXOLOTL

- Aquatic
- Grows to 8 to 11 inches (20 to 28 cm)
- Remains in the **larval** stage all of its life
- Comes in many colors, including gray, black, brown, white, and yellow
- Calmer than most other types of salamanders
- Almost **extinct** in nature

HELLBENDER

- Aquatic
- Grows to about 25 inches (63 cm) long
- Flat head and body with wrinkly skin
- Color is dull brown
- Can live for 30 years
- Does not like to live with other hellbenders; may bite
- Likes to walk along the bottom of an aquarium or stream

Salamander History

The earliest known salamanders lived about 150 million years ago during the Jurassic Period. Salamanders crawled and swam as dinosaurs walked the land.

Of all of the amphibians on Earth, salamanders have changed the least since ancient times. They are most like early amphibians. The hellbender salamander species closely resembles the **fossil** of a salamander that lived 8 million years ago. Today, there are about 380 different species of salamanders.

The name *salamander* is Greek. It means "fire-lizard." Ancient peoples believed that salamanders could walk through fire because they often crawled out from logs that had been thrown onto fires.

■ Scientists have found fossils of the earliest known salamanders in Mongolia and China.

Salamanders prefer to live in cool, moist environments. They are found throughout the northern part of the world. Their habitat stretches across the United States and Canada, extending south through Central America to the northern tip of South America. Salamanders also live in Europe, Asia, and northern parts of Africa.

Salamanders are very sensitive to heat. Their homes should be placed in a cool locations.

Fascinating Facts

- The salamander was the symbol of King Francois I of France. King Francois founded the French city of Le Havre. Le Havre's coat of arms features a salamander in flames.

9

Life Cycle

Salamanders go through many stages of growth. This process is called **metamorphosis**. Some types of salamanders go through these stages more quickly than others. For example, some salamanders are full-grown after a few months. Others take years to mature. The Mexican Axolotl never develops beyond the larval stage.

Eggs

Most female salamanders lay their eggs either on land or in water. Some females keep the eggs within their bodies and give birth to live young. The tiger salamander lays eggs in **clutches** of up to 500. The female leaves the eggs to hatch in streams and ponds. Other salamanders lay eggs in smaller clutches or one at a time. They may lay the eggs in hiding places, such as rotting logs. Females that lay small clutches usually protect their eggs from hungry **predators** until they hatch.

Mature

Different types salamanders do not look alike when they are adults. Some live on land. Others live in the water, or they may live both in water and on land. Most salamanders, with proper care, can live for a very long time.

Fascinating Facts

- Hellbenders can take up to five years to mature.
- Amphibians are the only animals with a backbone to go through metamorphosis.
- Newts lay their eggs one at a time. Females hide each egg from predators by wrapping it in a waterweed leaf.

Larvae

When salamanders hatch from their eggs, they are called larvae. During the larval stage, salamanders live in the water. They have feathery gills for breathing underwater. They look like tadpoles, which are frog larvae. For salamanders that give birth to live young, the larval stage happens inside the mother's body.

Metamorphosis

During metamorphosis, most larvae lose their gills and grow lungs for breathing on land. They also grow arms, legs, eyelids, and a tongue. For many larvae, metamorphosis lasts two or three months, but for some types, it can take years. Some species undergo a **partial** metamorphosis. They keep their gills to continue living underwater and grow lungs so they can also live on land. Other species never experience metamorphosis. They spend their entire life underwater.

Picking Your Pet

Choosing a pet salamander requires a great deal of thought. Gather as much information as you can about salamanders before making a decision. Caring properly for a pet that can live for many years is a big responsibility. Ask yourself some important questions before buying a salamander.

If a terrestrial salamander spends a great deal of time in the water bowl, the tank is probably too dry. Spray the tank with water from a spray bottle to add moisture.

Can I Provide a Good Home For a Salamander?

Salamanders need to be kept safe and happy in a closed tank that is cool and wet. It should be well ventilated to let in fresh air. The tank should also be kept in a dark place at night. It should not be in a room where there are lights that are turned on often. Salamanders do not like to be disturbed. Their tank should be located in a quiet place. They should not be placed where someone might bump into the tank or tap on the glass.

■ Rough skinned newts live along the west coast of the United States and Canada.

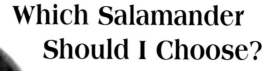

Which Salamander Should I Choose?

Salamanders come in different sizes. To care for a large salamander, such as the hellbender, you must make sure that you have a big tank. You will also need to clear a large space in your home for the tank. Smaller salamanders, such as fire salamanders, can live as long as 50 years. You must be prepared to care for your pet for the entire length of its life.

Newts are a type of small salamander that spend most of their life on land.

How Much Does a Salamander Cost?

The more common types of pet salamanders, such as newts, are not expensive. However, salamanders need a tank, plants, rocks, and food. Look into the cost of supplies needed to house, feed, and care for a salamander before you purchase your pet.

Fascinating Facts

- Salamanders make very little noise. They sometimes make small sounds, such as squeaks, coughs, or grunts.
- Like lizards, salamanders can lose their tails if they are handled roughly. However, the tail will grow back.
- Salamanders are nocturnal. Nocturnal animals are most active at night.

Salamander Supplies

All pet salamanders need an enclosure. The type of enclosure depends on the type of salamander. Aquatic salamanders live in the water and need an aquarium. Terrestrial salamanders live on land and need a terrarium. Both terrariums and aquariums are glass tanks that come in many sizes. Larger salamanders will need a bigger tank than smaller salamanders. The tank should have a lid to prevent the salamander from escaping.

■ Many terrestrial salamander owners grow moss in their terrariums to provide extra moisture.

Line the bottom of the salamander's tank with some type of **substrate**. For aquatic salamanders, gravel is the best substrate to use. Gravel can be bought at a pet store. Gravel can also be used as a substrate for terrestrial salamanders. However, soil is a better choice because live plants can be added to a soil-filled terrarium. Every terrarium also needs a bowl of water where the salamander can soak and stay wet.

Both aquatic and terrestrial salamanders need living or plastic plants inside their tank. They also require large rocks to hide behind or under. Some salamanders like to lie on top of a flat rock.

Unbleached, wet paper towels can make a good substrate layer in a temporary shelter.

Fascinating Facts

• Terrariums can be kept **humid** by placing plastic food wrap over the top of the tank and poking a few small holes in the top. Remove the wrap every few days and spray the tank with water from a spray bottle.

Salamander Snacks

Most salamanders are carnivores. This means they eat meat. Aquatic salamanders use their sense of smell to find food. They eat by opening their mouth in the water and sucking in food. Terrestrial salamanders use their sense of sight to find food. They roll their sticky tongue out of their mouth, wait for their **prey** to come within reach, and snatch up their meal.

It is easy to provide a salamander with a healthy, varied diet. Salamanders eat tadpoles, worms, shrimp, bugs, and small fish. Although they prefer live food, some salamanders will eat food that has been frozen and thawed.

Vitamins help salamanders stay healthy. Sprinkle vitamin powder on a salamander's food.

■ Pet salamanders should not eat insects that have been caught outdoors. They may have been exposed to harmful chemicals that can make the salamander ill.

Fascinating Facts

- The tongue of some tropical salamanders is nearly as long as their body.
- In nature, when the weather is too cold or too dry for salamanders to search for food, they enter a resting state similar to **hibernation**.
- Small strips of beef are a special treat for pet salamanders. However, because beef is high in fat, it should not be fed to salamanders often.

Young salamanders should be fed every day. Adult salamanders only need to be fed every three to five days. Salamanders will not overeat. They will only eat until they are full, leaving some food behind.

Although salamanders rarely drink water, it is very important that they have a fresh supply at all times. Like all amphibians, salamanders need to keep their skin wet. Sometimes they might swallow a little water when eating underwater.

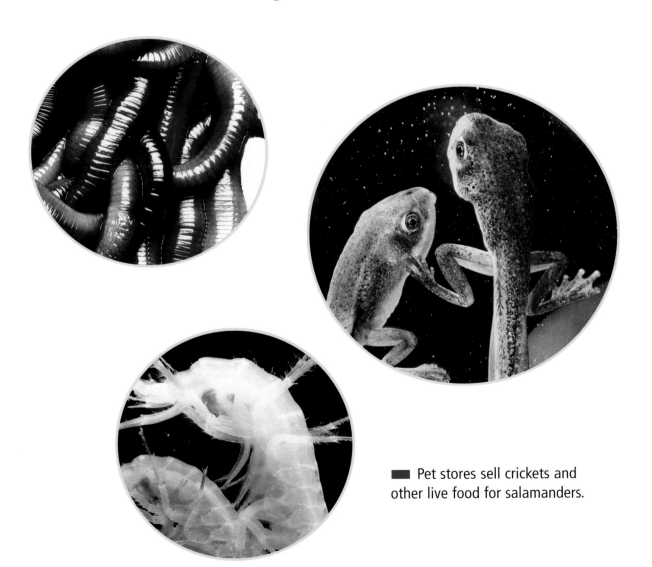

■ Pet stores sell crickets and other live food for salamanders.

Tail and Toes

Although salamanders may look like lizards, they have features that set them apart. Unlike lizards, salamanders do not have scales or claws. Their special features are suited to their natural moist environment. Understanding those features will help you create a home that suits your pet's needs.

■ **SALAMANDER**

Salamanders are the only adult amphibians that have a long tail. They use their tail for balance when walking and to help them swim. If a predator threatens, a salamander can shed its tail. This distracts the predator while the salamander escapes.

Salamanders have soft fingers and toes. The fingers and toes of aquatic salamanders are often webbed to help them swim.

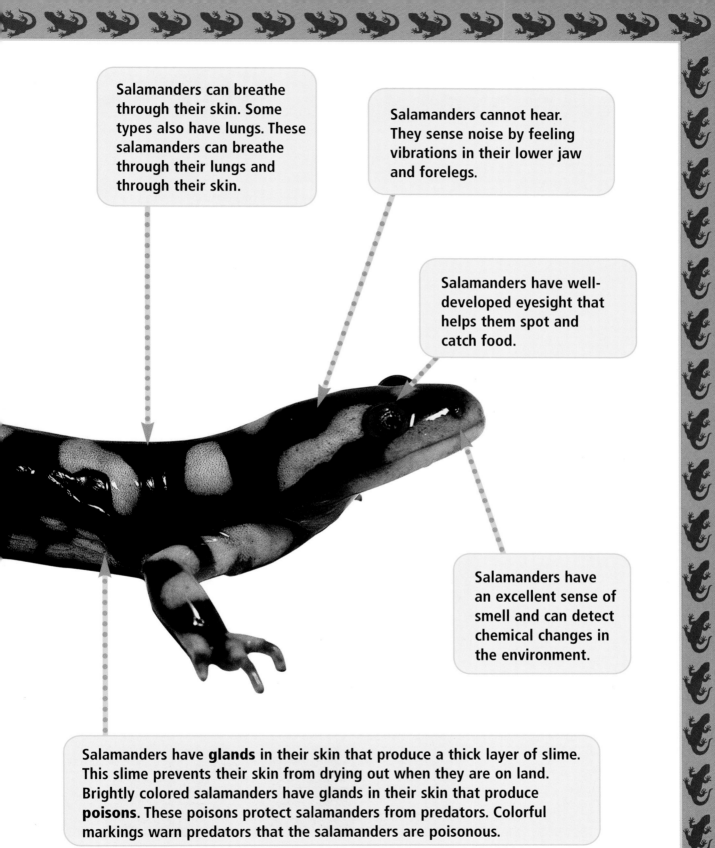

Salamanders can breathe through their skin. Some types also have lungs. These salamanders can breathe through their lungs and through their skin.

Salamanders cannot hear. They sense noise by feeling vibrations in their lower jaw and forelegs.

Salamanders have well-developed eyesight that helps them spot and catch food.

Salamanders have an excellent sense of smell and can detect chemical changes in the environment.

Salamanders have **glands** in their skin that produce a thick layer of slime. This slime prevents their skin from drying out when they are on land. Brightly colored salamanders have glands in their skin that produce **poisons**. These poisons protect salamanders from predators. Colorful markings warn predators that the salamanders are poisonous.

Salamander Stress

Salamanders do not enjoy being handled, so it is not a good idea to touch or play with your pet. Handling salamanders causes them stress, which might make them bite. The bites are not deadly, but they can be painful. The hellbender has a very painful bite.

When moving a pet salamander, gently nudge it into a temporary container, rather than pick it up in your hands.

A red eft is a young eastern newt. Efts live on land.

Salamanders should be observed in the same way as fish—by watching them frolic inside their tank. If you want to play with your pet, you should consider choosing a different type of animal.

It is important to try not to touch the poisonous skin of colorful salamanders. If you must touch or pick up a salamander, make sure to wash your hands afterward. Do not put your hands near your eyes or mouth because you could become ill.

■ It is a good idea to clean your hands with soap after handling a salamander.

Fascinating Facts

- Adult mud puppies can go for more than a month with very little food if they are living in cold water.
- A type of salamander called the olm lives its entire life in total darkness. Olms live in caves. Although they have eyes, they are completely blind.

Healthy and Happy

Pet salamanders often do not eat when you first bring them to their new home. This does not mean that they are ill. They likely are just becoming familiar their surroundings. They may be under too much stress to hunt for food. Keep the salamander in a dark place, and leave it alone until it adjusts to its new home.

Most tap water contains a chemical called chlorine. Tap water must be **dechlorinated** before adding it to a salamander's tank. This can be done by letting it sit at room temperature for at least 24 hours or by adding a **water conditioner** sold at pet stores.

A salamander's tank should be cleaned often. Keeping the tank clean will help the salamander remain healthy and happy. A dirty tank can make a salamander ill.

Some salamanders prefer to live alone. Be sure your salamander species gets along well with other salamanders before putting more than one in a cage.

■ If a newt loses a limb, a new one will grow in its place.

A filter can help keep the water in an aquarium clean. Filters can be bought at a pet store. Without a filter, the water in an aquarium should be changed every three days.

To clean the tank, place the salamander in a temporary container with some water. The container should have a lid with small holes in the top so the salamander can breathe. Remove rocks, plants, and substrate from the tank. Clean the tank thoroughly. Make sure to thoroughly rinse any soap from the aquarium before refilling the tank.

■ Spotted salamanders spend most of the year underground or hiding under forest litter.

Fascinating Facts

- Salamanders like a clean home. They cannot survive in a polluted environment.
- The crested newt is on the protected species list in Great Britain. At one time, many crested newts lived in Europe, but the chemicals farmers used to kill crop-eating insects also killed crested newts.

Salamander Behavior

Salamanders prefer to be left alone. They do not need other salamanders for company. In fact, some types of salamanders do not get along with each other. Before you decide to get more than one salamander, make sure that they enjoy being around other salamanders.

In nature, a salamander may only travel 1 mile (1.6 kilometers) in its entire lifetime.

■ Many salamanders enjoy swimming, but some prefer living on the land and will avoid ponds and streams.

Pet Peeves

Salamanders do not like
- people tapping on the glass of their tank
- being handled
- dirty water
- bright lights

Salamanders sleep during the day. They move around and hunt for prey at night. Salamanders are very good at hiding, so it is sometimes difficult to spot a salamander in its cage. Some terrestrial salamanders **burrow** into soil, while others hide behind plants or under rocks.

If a salamander has a quick **pulsing** in its throat, the temperature likely is too hot. When a salamander is moving in a fast or jerky manner, the animal may be under stress. A salamander that seems sick or under stress may need to visit a **veterinarian**.

If a Mexican axolotl's gills are moving quickly, it is possible that the animal is not getting enough oxygen. To fix this, replace the water in the tank with clean water.

■ A salamander's body temperature depends on its environment. Sometimes, a salamander will bask in sunlight to keep warm.

Fascinating Facts

- Salamanders shed their skin. They often eat their old skin.
- Salamanders may attack other salamanders. Bigger salamanders are known to eat smaller salamanders.

Salamander Stories

Salamanders have long been connected with evil and mischief. In fairy tales, witches made magic potions from many strange ingredients, including the eyes and tails of salamanders.

According to popular folklore in the past, salamanders would drink milk from cows they found lying down in fields. Afterward, the cows would not be able to produce any more milk. As a result, whenever a cow could not produce milk, a salamander was blamed.

■ The three witches in Shakespeare's play *Macbeth* needed an "eye of newt" to complete a magic potion.

Fascinating Facts

- In the past, the hellbender's bite was believed to be poisonous, earning it the nickname "devil dog".

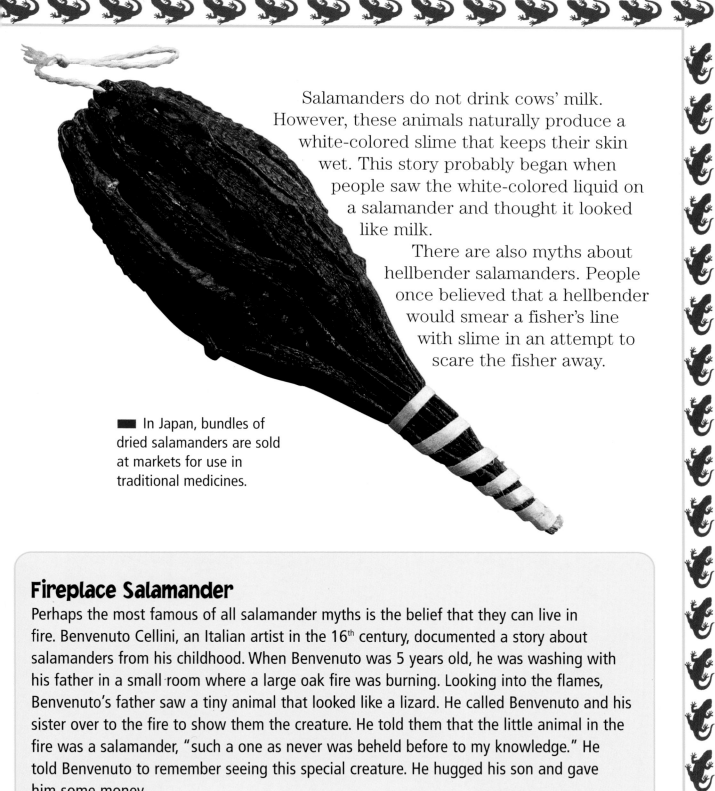

Salamanders do not drink cows' milk. However, these animals naturally produce a white-colored slime that keeps their skin wet. This story probably began when people saw the white-colored liquid on a salamander and thought it looked like milk.

There are also myths about hellbender salamanders. People once believed that a hellbender would smear a fisher's line with slime in an attempt to scare the fisher away.

■ In Japan, bundles of dried salamanders are sold at markets for use in traditional medicines.

Fireplace Salamander

Perhaps the most famous of all salamander myths is the belief that they can live in fire. Benvenuto Cellini, an Italian artist in the 16th century, documented a story about salamanders from his childhood. When Benvenuto was 5 years old, he was washing with his father in a small room where a large oak fire was burning. Looking into the flames, Benvenuto's father saw a tiny animal that looked like a lizard. He called Benvenuto and his sister over to the fire to show them the creature. He told them that the little animal in the fire was a salamander, "such a one as never was beheld before to my knowledge." He told Benvenuto to remember seeing this special creature. He hugged his son and gave him some money.

Pet Puzzlers

How much do you know about salamanders? Test your knowledge by answering the following questions.

Q Do salamanders like to be held?

Salamanders do not like to be held or touched.

Q What do salamanders like to eat?

Salamanders like to eat live food, including larvae, worms, shrimp, bugs, and small fish. They also like small strips of beef.

Q What is the difference between an aquatic salamander and a terrestrial salamander?

Aquatic salamanders live underwater. Terrestrial salamanders live on land.

Q What should be inside a terrestrial salamander's tank?

Plants, rocks, substrate, and a water dish should be in the tank of a terrestrial salamander.

Q Are salamanders harmful to humans?

Salamanders are not harmful to humans, but they need to be treated with special care. Salamanders can bite, and some have skin that is poisonous to touch.

Q Can more than one salamander live together?

Only some types of salamanders can live together. It is important to find out which kinds of salamanders are friendly.

Q Can fire salamanders live in fire?

The belief that fire salamanders are fireproof is a myth.

Salamander Names

Before you buy your pet salamander, write down some salamander names that you like. Some names may work better for a female salamander. Others may suit a male salamander. Here are a few suggestions.

Splash

Digger

Spot

Dragon

Slick

Sally

Tiger

Flames

Peter Pan

Frequently Asked Questions

My salamander escaped. What should I do?

Look in every dark place in the house, including the vents. If you do not find the salamander, put pieces of tin foil filled with water in every room of the house so that your salamander can stay wet. You may be able to hear your pet crawl onto the foil.

I found a salamander outside. Can I keep it?

It is not a good idea to catch and keep wild salamanders. Many are protected by laws in an effort to keep salamanders alive in nature. You may not be able to identify what type of salamander you have caught. You would not know the right temperature, foods, and habitat that type of salamander needs. Therefore, you could not care for it properly.

I do not want my salamander anymore. What should I do?

Do not let the salamander free outdoors. It will not be able to survive in nature. Releasing a pet into nature can also be bad for the environment. The salamander may carry diseases that could kill local animals or plants. It is **illegal** to abandon pets, so try finding a new owner. Take the salamander to a pet store, place an ad in the newspaper, or take it to a pet rescue society.

More Information

Animal Organizations

You can help salamanders stay healthy and happy by learning more about them. Many organizations are dedicated to teaching people how to care for and protect their pet pals. For more salamander information, e-mail the following organizations:

Museum of Comparative Zoology
Harvard University
26 Oxford Street
Cambridge, MA 02318

Department of Biological Sciences
The Open University, Walton Hall
Milton Keynes
Mk7 6AA United Kingdom

Websites

To answer more of your salamander questions, visit the following websites:

Declining Amphibian Populations Task Force
www.open.ac.uk/daptf

Livingunderworld.org
www.livingunderworld.org

Words to Know

burrow: to dig into the ground
clutches: sets of eggs
cold-blooded: having a body temperature that changes with the surroundings
dechlorinated: to remove the chemical chlorine from water
extinct: no longer living any place on Earth
fossil: rocklike remains of ancient plants or animals
glands: organs that produce a fluid or chemicals necessary to the body
hibernation: to spend a period of time in a sleep-like state
humid: wet or damp environment
illegal: against the law
larval: the newly hatched first stage of life for amphibians before metamorphosis

metamorphosis: a change of form and appearance
partial: affecting only part
poisons: substances that can make animals and people ill
predators: animals that hunt and kill other animals for food
prey: animals that are hunted and eaten by other animals
pulsing: movement caused by a quick heartbeat
substrate: the surface on which a salamander lives
veterinarian: animal doctor
water conditioner: a substance that removes chlorine from water

Index